IRAN:

CYBER REPRESSION

How the IRGC Uses Cyberwarfare To Preserve the Theocracy

Published by

National Council of Resistance of Iran
U.S. Representative Office

IRAN: CYBER REPRESSION; How the IRGC Uses Cyberwarfare To Preserve the Theocracy

Copyright © National Council of Resistance of Iran – U.S. Representative Office, 2018.

All rights reserved. No part of this monograph may be used or reproduced in any manner whatsoever without written permission except in the case of brief quotations embodied in articles or reviews.

First published in 2018 by

National Council of Resistance of Iran - U.S. Representative Office (NCRI-US), 1747 Pennsylvania Ave., NW, Suite 1125, Washington, DC 20006

ISBN: 978-1-944942-13-7

ISBN: 978-1-944942-14-4 (e-book)

Library of Congress Control Number: 2018933666

Library of Congress Cataloging-in-Publication Data

National Council of Resistance of Iran - U.S. Representative Office.

IRAN: CYBER REPRESSION; How the IRGC Uses Cyberwarfare To Preserve the Theocracy

1.Iran. 2. Cyber. 3. Human Rights. 4. Social Media. 5.Internet. 6.Revolutionary Guards

First Edition: February 2018

Printed in the United States of America

These materials are being distributed by the National Council of Resistance of Iran-U.S. Representative Office. Additional information is on file with the Department of Justice, Washington, D.C.

TABLE OF CONTENTS

Executive Summary 5

Background 9

Iran Uprising in the Digital Age 17

IRGC's Cyberwarfare
    A New Wave of Cyber Repression 23
    IRGC's Front Companies & Apps 27
    Key players in Iran's latest cyberwarfare 43
    Ammar base Cyberspace organizational chart 44
    IRGC Intelligence Organization chart 45

Policy Recommendations: Countermeasures to
Cyber Repression in Iran 49

APPENDIX 51

Glossary of Terms 63

About NCRI-US 65

List of Publications 66

EXECUTIVE SUMMARY

The latest popular uprising in Iran against the ruling theocracy erupted on December 28, 2017 and spread to 142 towns and cities with breakneck speed. The protests sent shockwaves inside the regime and around the world. Many policy experts now view the uprising as a "landmark event" and a "turning point" since the regime's establishment in 1979.

Protesters make game-changing use of cyber-technology: The use of technology, mobile devices and social messaging platforms played a significant role in helping the protesters to organize, exchange information between different locales, and get their message out to the rest of the world. The protesters' use of cyber technology proved to be the regime's Achilles' Heel since it could not, despite a huge show of force, stop the expansion of protests. Starting the second day, the protests, with pre-announced locations and time, expanded even as the regime desperately cut off access to the Internet and blocked key mobile apps such as Telegram at considerable financial and political cost as well as international embarrassment.

IRGC elevates domestic cyberwarfare: A new wave of domestic cyberwarfare, led by the Islamic Revolutionary Guard Corps (IRGC) in collaboration with the Ministry of Intelligence and Security (MOIS), accelerated significantly after the eruption of the nationwide protests. The internal network of the main opposition People's Mojahedin Organization of Iran (MEK/PMOI), which is the principal member of the National

Council of Resistance of Iran (NCRI), has established that the regime has focused on mass surveillance through malicious codes embedded in IRGC mobile apps to actively monitor and disrupt the communication of protesters and dissidents.

Regime's domestic cyberwarfare shifts focus from access control to stateful endpoint surveillance: With the recent uprising, the Iranian regime is now complementing its network surveillance with stateful endpoint (mobile device) monitoring of content, context and contacts to counter the expansion of the uprising and to avert more protests.

MEK sources: IRGC establishes domestic mobile apps marketplace to spread spyware enabled apps: The homegrown market place, ***Café Bazaar***, modeled after Google Play, is supervised by the IRGC. It is the IRGC's platform of choice to promote and distribute spyware enabled mobile apps.

MEK sources: IRGC front companies are developing spyware-enabled apps for cyber-surveillance and repression: Through front companies, such as ***Hanista***, the IRGC has created apps such as ***Mobogram***, an unofficial **Telegram** fork. Ironically, some of these spyware-enabled apps are available on Google Play, Apple Store, and GitHub, potentially exposing millions of users worldwide to the IRGC's spyware and surveillance activities.

Iran's universities have become a recruiting ground for IRGC cyberwarfare personnel. All recruits are hired through front companies that often engage in "research" activities with a few of the IRGC's "handpicked professors." These companies identify the needed talent for cyberwarfare. Many of these recruits leave once they discover the companies' links to the IRGC.

Foreign Assistance: Tehran has used foreign assistance to advance its cyberwarfare. On September 4, 2012, state-run Fars News Agency reported, "signing of an agreement between Iran and North Korea to confront cyber attacks has raised concerns in the west." Tehran has also benefitted from significant assistance from Lebanon. Using its influence on Hezbollah, the Iranian regime has gained access to Lebanese security apparatus for its cyberwarfare against the Iranian people as well as fulfilling its objectives to counter the west.

Regime's IRGC-led domestic cyberwarfare violates Article 19 of the Universal Declaration of Human Rights: In line with the regime's attempts to ensure its survival, the domestic cyberwarfare targets its number one enemy: the Iranian people and their movement for democracy. The regime's cyberwarfare is a vivid manifestation of cyber repression and constitutes a grave violation of Article 19 of the Universal Declaration of Human Rights.

Access to free, safe and secure Internet is now a new battleground pitting the people against the regime. Data shows nearly 48 million Iranians have smartphones and about 70% have access to the Internet. As the call for freedom and regime change grows louder in Iran, it is crucial to understand how the international community could stand on the side of the democracy movement by implementing effective measures to curb and confront the regime's cyberspace repression of the Iranian people.

BACKGROUND

As early as 1990s, Tehran was concerned about the impact of the Internet. In a October 8, 1996 story in the New York Times, Iranian officials expressed their fear, "'The brains of the young are very impressionable, so the Mujahedeen Khalq (MEK) might be able to brainwash people to join them, or they might be able to influence an election,' said a senior Government official familiar with the Internet project."[1]

Tehran's fear of Internet became a reality in May 2001 when the regime's supreme leader, Ali Khamenei, personally intervened to confront the public's growing political awareness as a result of access to the Internet. Under a plan called "Broad Policies for the World Wide Web," he ordered that access to the Internet must only be allowed through institutions permitted by the regime. Following the order, in October 2001, the *Supreme Cultural Council of the Revolution* chaired by then-president Mohammad Khatami, adopted a resolution for content censorship entitled "Regulations and Rules Related to the World Wide Web," which called for government control over Application Service Providers (ASP).

In December 2002, the *Committee to Prescribe Measures against Prohibited Internet Bases* was formed, and included representatives from the Intelligence Ministry, Ministry of Islamic Guidance, Ministry of Communications and Technology, and the Judiciary. It determined criteria according to which,

---

1. "With Mixed Feelings, Iran Tiptoes to the Internet," Neil MacFarquahr, The New York Times, October 8, 1996, http://www.nytimes.com/1996/10/08/world/with-mixed-feelings-iran-tiptoes-to-the-internet.html

by March 2003 (in three months), over 15,000 websites were blacklisted and filtered. In 2003, the *Supreme Council for Information Sharing Security* was formed to set cyber policies. Chaired at a vice president level, its members include the secretary of the *Supreme National Security Council*, the chairman of the armed forces chiefs of staff, the intelligence minister, the minister of communication, and the minister of Islamic guidance. The presence of the secretary of the *Supreme National Security Council* and the intelligence minister indicates the intense focus on censorship and cyber repression coupled with wider domestic suppression, and foreign and domestic espionage. The role of the chairman of the joint chiefs is related to leveraging the cyber force for the military programs, especially missile and nuclear programs. The role of the Islamic guidance minister indicates the broader coordination of the regime's activities on the ground and in cyberspace at home and abroad.

In 2005, the *Supreme Council for Technological Innovation* was formed and chaired by the regime's president. The Council had 14 members, including ministers, deputy ministers and the head of the main state-run broadcaster. Its mandate was to set the strategic policies for technological advancement. With former regime president Mahmoud Ahmadinejad as the chair of the Council, a mandate was given to the communications ministry to censor and suppress under the banner of "clearing out illegal content," "identifying users that violate the law," and "monitoring anti-regime websites." IRGC's power was increasingly consolidated during Ahmadinejad's tenure and in 2007 the first coordinated IRGC effort in cyberwarfare for domestic suppression and combating opposition sites was launched. According to IRGC's training material, "the cultural war is a serious threat to the regime. Since the IRGC's core responsibilities include confronting all enemy threats against the essence of the regime, the IRGC has a duty to intervene in this regard."[2]

---

2. Report by the National Council of Resistance of Iran about the Iranian Regime's Cyber Army, April 2016, https://www.ncriran.org/en/news/exclusive-reports/20114-ncri-publishes-report-on-iran-s-cyber-army

On November 21, 2010, Brigadier General Hossein Hamedani, the commander of the Mohammad Rasulollah base in Greater Tehran, announced: "The Bassij cyber council has trained over 1,500 cyber warriors who are now active." He added that such activities would be stepped up soon. IRGC claims to have reached "the second [strongest] cyber army in the world."[3]

Tehran has used foreign assistance to advance its cyberwarfare. On September 4, 2012, state-run Fars News Agency reported, "signing of an agreement between Iran and North Korea to confront cyber attacks has raised concerns in the west." Tehran has also benefitted from significant assistance from Lebanon. Using its influence on Hezbollah, the Iranian regime has gained access to Lebanese security apparatus for its cyberwarfare against the Iranian people as well as fulfilling its objective to counter the west.

For a full assessment and understanding of the Iranian regime's cyber threat, one must examine the nature of the theocracy, and the elements that motivate or deter this regime. The ongoing uprising in Iran has shown the world community that the Iranian regime is more fearful of its own people and their desire for freedom than any foreign power.

Free, safe and secure access to the Internet is now the new battleground between the people of Iran and the ruling regime. The Iranian regime fears the 48 million mobile devices currently in the hands of people who are creatively and relentlessly finding new ways to get their unfiltered message of #IranProtests, #BanIRIB, or #FreeIran to the rest of the world. The clarity contained in the message of the nationwide uprising, marked by chants of "down with Khamenei and Rouhani," has unmasked the regime,

---

3. "1,500 Cyber Warriors Trained by Bassij," State-affiliated Tabnak, November 21, 2010. (Translated from Farsi), http://www.tabnak.ir/fa/news/131929/

be it in cyber space or in towns across Iran. It is within this context that we can examine the regime's cyber repression and the role of the IRGC in developing new cyber threats and attacks at home and abroad.

Since 2012, there has been many reports indicating how the Iranian regime is investing in cyber technology, infrastructure and training. Some have argued Iran is "emerging as a significant cyberthreat to the US and its allies."[4]

Undoubtedly, the regime continues to expand the scope of its cyberwarfare at home and abroad and the IRGC and the Ministry of Intelligence and Security (MOIS) have been at the center of these effort.[5] These entities have been engaged in cyberwarfare since 2007, and increasingly elevated their efforts after the 2009 uprisings.

These endeavors target domestic opponents and are used to launch attacks against foes abroad. In 2016, the National Council of Resistance of Iran published its first Cyber Report on the "cyber army" established under the direction of IRGC commander Mohammad-Ali Jafari. "The regime's Supreme National Security Council has adopted decisions for the cyber army to confront and institute measures against websites abroad, and to monitor and act against Internet threats against the regime within Iran," the report said.

While sanctions have hampered the Iranian regime's ability to fully arm its Cyber Army with all the necessary and modern tools, infrastructure and skills, IRGC has been able to elevate its attacks against targets in the US, Canada, Middle East and Europe, going beyond just defacing and

---

4. Frederick W. Kagan and Tommy Stiansen, "The growing cyberthreat from Iran: The initial report of Project Pistachio Harvest," American Enterprise Institute Critical Threats Project and Norse Corporation, April 2015, http://www.aei.org/publication/growing-cyberthreat-from-iran/

5. The Ministry of Intelligence and Security (MOIS) is the primary intelligence agency of the Iranian regime. It is also known by its Farsi acronym VEVAK (Vezarat-e Ettela'at va Amniat-e Keshvar).

DDoS (distributed denial of service) attacks. Industry and media reports by leading cyber forensic and intelligence companies have documented the Iranian regime's efforts on malware development, more sophisticated social engineering and phishing attacks.

The focus of this report, however, is to demonstrate how the regime, under the supervision and guidance of IRGC and MOIS, continues to employ new tactics and techniques against the people of Iran, in a desperate attempt to counter the growing dissent inside the country, and in particular the recent nationwide uprising, which began on December 28, 2017.

The Iranian regime is among a very few governments in the world where its testbed of cyberattacks and strategies is its own citizens. Experiments, test and optimization of IRGC's cyberattacks on Iranians before deploying elsewhere is in line with Tehran's longstanding worldview of instilling fear and repression at home while promoting terrorism, Islamic fundamentalism and chaos abroad. After all, a regime that fears its citizens' free access to the Internet, conducts cyber spying on internal political factions and its citizens, along with practices that result in intimidation, blackmailing, disruption, and destruction, is inherently weak, unstable and vulnerable.

The regime's paranoia leads to intense cyber operations run by the IRGC and MOIS that focuses on creating a fake impression of dramatic improvements in nurturing homegrown talent and capacity to advance the regime's cyberwarfare. At the same time, we must not underestimate the regime's inherent need for repression, including cyber repression, when it comes to the Iranian society. It is within this context that we can understand the regime's increased investment in cyber technology.

Since 2008, the Iranian regime has invested in western technology and provided technical requirements to several European and Asian companies to "analyze all messages in English, Persian or Arabic for keywords or phrases; store them; and flag those caught by filters for review." Other specific requirements explicitly requested the ability "to change the content of messages."[6]

Understanding what motivates the Iranian regime to unleash extraordinary cyber repression on the people of Iran can help secure an essential foundation for the Information Society everywhere. As outlined in Article 19 of the Universal Declaration of Human Rights, everyone has the right to freedom of opinion and expression; and this right includes freedom to hold opinions without interference and to seek, receive and impart information and ideas through any media regardless of frontiers. "Communication is a fundamental social process, a basic human need and the foundation of all social organization. It is central to the Information Society. Everyone, everywhere should have the opportunity to participate and no one should be excluded from the benefits the Information Society offers."[7] The Iranian people should be no exception and that the struggle and plight for securing their digital rights and protection should be a global struggle.

To demystify cyber talent, one cannot deny that Iran's nation has proudly produced some of the brightest minds who have contributed significantly to advancement of knowledge and technological progress worldwide. Yet, it is a fallacy to think Iran's top cyber talent is at the service of the IRGC. It is true that Iran's universities have become a recruiting ground for IRGC cyberwarfare. According to MEK's sources inside Iran, thus far,

---

6. Ben Elgin, Vernon Silver and Alan Katz, "Iranian Police Seizing Dissidents Get Aid Of Western Companies," Bloomberg, October 30, 2011, https://www.bloomberg.com/news/articles/2011-10-31/iranian-police-seizing-dissidents-get-aid-of-western-companies

7. "Declaration of Principles Building the Information Society: a global challenge in the new Millennium," Work Summit on the Information Society, December 12, 2003, https://www.itu.int/net/wsis/docs/geneva/official/dop.html

recruits have been hired through front companies, which often engage in "research" activities with a few of the IRGC's "handpicked professors" and identify the needed talent for cyberwarfare.

Within the first few months, the majority of these recruits leave these companies after they realize that they are linked to the IRGC. Others end up staying after being threatened or intimidated.[8] The IRGC has not been able to attract and retain top talent for its cyber repression and warfare. It is for this reason that in 2014, the IRGC's Brigadier General, Seyed Masoud Jazayeri, called for "national mobilization against the Internet threat," inviting "youths, university students and professors, [to] strive to confront the enemies' threats and thwart their plots."[9] The Iranian people believe any support for the IRGC's cyberwarfare agenda is unpatriotic and contrary to their nationalistic pride and values. A few cyber thugs at the service of the IRGC will not define the Iranian nation's rightful place in cyber space.

8. Two high profile members of the regime's cyber army were murdered to instill fear in others. Mohammad Hussein Tajik, the manager of the IRGC cyber army was killed in his home in July 2016. In 2013, Mojtaba Ahmadi, commander of the Cyber War Headquarters was found dead in a woodland near the city of Karaj.

9. "Commander Calls for Concerted Efforts to Counter Soft War against Iran," IRGC-affiliated Tasnim, January 11, 2014. https://www.tasnimnews.com/en/news/2014/01/11/246507/commander-calls-for-concerted-efforts-to-counter-soft-war-against-iran

IRAN UPRISING IN THE DIGITAL AGE

With the recent uprising, the Iranian people put an end to the myth of "reformers" vs. "hardliners" inside the regime. The same holds true for cyber activities of the Iranian regime. The regime in its entirety is unified in its strategy for cyber repression of the Iranian people. The structure of the councils with direct oversight on ministries, intelligence officers as key technical decision makers, telecom infrastructure and operators, Internet Service Providers (ISP's) and user's mobile connectivity is all geared toward meeting the IRGC's full control over all content, behavior and activities on the Internet. Iran's president, Hassan Rouhani, claims to be advocating for public access to the Internet, but in reality he is unmistakably advocating to balance popular demand for Internet access with the requirements of cyber repression at the service of supreme leader, Ali Khamenei, and the IRGC.

Protesters use their mobile devices during the uprising

On January 26, 2018, Ahmad Jannati, the head of the regime's Assembly of Experts announced that "the leader (Khamenei) had a meeting with a number of cyberspace specialists for a few hours on Tuesday (January 23) and had serious talks about this issue" adding "cyberspace is a blow to our life." Ahmad Khatami, spokesman for the Assembly of Experts, told reporters "All the attendees at the meeting (Assembly of Experts' Commissions) were worried about cyberspace and explicitly said that the administrators of the recent turmoil (unrests) were cyberspace seditionists."[10]

Khamenei: "Cyber space is as important as the Islamic Revolution"

Millions of Iranians have access to the Internet and over 48 million own smartphones. Iran's young and restless population has become increasingly tech savvy over the years to evade the regime's controls, censorship and speed limitations. The continuous cyber resistance by the public has driven the regime to route Internet traffic through one of the state-controlled systems, making it very difficult for any subscriber to evade state-sponsored cyber repression.[11]

Supreme Leader Ali Khamenei is on the record giving high priority to contain the cyber threat to the regime. "Cyber space is as important as the

---

10. "Iran Regime's Mullahs: If Cyberspace Left Unrestrained, It Will Be Problematic Again", January 27, 2018 https://ncr-iran.org/ en/news/iran-protests/24237-iran-regime-s-mullahs-if-cyberspace-left-unrestrained-it-will-be-problematic-again

11. "Internet Filtering in Iran in 2004-2005: A Country Study," OpenNet Initiative. https://opennet.net/studies/iran#toc2c

Islamic Revolution," said Khamenei.[12] He is also widely quoted as saying, "If I were not the Leader of the Revolution, I would have definitely become the chief of cyber space."[13]

In 2004, OpenNet Initiative conducted a research on Internet filtering in Iran and concluded "Iran has adopted one of the world's most substantial Internet censorship regimes." The report also pointed to "use of the filtering product" such as "Smart filter, developed by a United States-based for-profit corporation" and raised "questions about the complicity of western commercial firms in the filtering regimes of non-democratic countries."[14]

During the 2009 uprising, the Wall Street Journal reported on how the "regime has developed, with the assistance of European telecommunications companies, one of the world's most sophisticated mechanisms for controlling and censoring the Internet, allowing it to examine the content of individual online communications on a massive scale."[15]

Over the years, the Iranian regime has gone beyond just blocking and filtering technology to content control, deep packet inspection, data alteration and user behavioral analytics to expand its cyber repression at home. While the advancement of Iran's telecom, data, WIFI and mobile infrastructure has afforded the Iranian people the opportunity to creatively connect with the outside world and convey their desire for freedom and democracy, the Iranian regime is hard at work utilizing new tactics and techniques to reign in the Internet freedom. With the launch of regime-controlled network, "Halal Internet", the Iranian regime gained a new

---

12. Photo Title, Defa Press, January 17, 2017, http://defapress.ir/fa/news/222236/
13. "If I weren't the leader," Harfeto website, August 6, 2017, http://harfeto.ir/News/25138.html
14. Ibid.
15. Christopher Rhoads and Loretta Chao, "Iran's Web Spying Aided By Western Technology," The Wall Street Journal, June 22, 2009. https://www.wsj.com/articles/SB124562668777335653

lever to control connectivity of the country with the rest of the world.[16]

In response to the rapid spread of the uprising that began in late December 2017, the Supreme Council on Cyberspace and the IRGC decided to briefly cut off Iran's access to the global Internet while keeping the "Halal Internet" up and running.[17] The regime's next move was to curb the spread of uprising through blocking of the popular social media apps such as Telegram serving nearly 40 million users in Iran.[18]

Supreme Leader Ali Khamenei meeting with members of Supreme Council on Cyberspace

Iran's National Security Council – a subcommittee of Supreme National Security Council – made the decision to block Telegram on December 31, 2017.

On January 7, 2018, the Iranian regime moved to unblock Telegram. The Iranian regime's Minister of Information and Communication Technology, Mohammad Javad Azari Jahromi, tweeted "I feel duty-bound to apologize to hundreds of thousands of my compatriots who have incurred losses due

---

16. The "Halal Internet" is also known as the National Information Network (NIN)
17. A similar action was taken during the 2009 uprising that caused significant disruption for the regime's own operations. With Halal Internet in place in 2017, the disruption was less, yet the regime was still not able to keep Iran off the international grid for too long.
18. "Telegram in Dilemma over Keeping One Channel or 40 Million Users," Iran Front Page, January 2, 2018, http://ifpnews.com/ exclusive/telegram-dilemma-keeping-one-channel-40-million-users/

to the existing conditions," referring to the blocking of Telegram and the losses incurred on those who use the platform for their businesses. Acknowledging the need to remain connected on the Internet as a nation, he added: "As one of its [Iran's] plans to counter the issue of unemployment, the government has supported, and will support the development of start-ups and reinforcement of the cyberspace."

What Jahromi did not share publicly was the IRGC's move to impose speed limitations and connection throttling for Telegram users and escalated campaign for promoting homegrown apps that allows the IRGC full surveillance control. On January 16, 2017, Pavel Durov, the founder of Telegram, acknowledged the diminished speed of access to Telegram.

In this report, NCRI-US reveals information about the regime's new wave of cyber repression, key players behind the new wave of cyberwarfare, while offering a political context to enrich the current discourse on the Iranian regime's cyber threat. The report also exposes the regime's latest plans to use fake mobile apps as weapons against protesters and mobile users inside and outside of Iran.[19]

---

19. For the purpose of this report, we define "fake apps" as applications that piggyback on the names, designs or functions of more popular apps in an attempt to trick users into downloading them. In Iran's case, most fake apps have been designed and named based on the popular messaging platform Telegram, which offers speed and security to users.

A NEW WAVE OF CYBER REPRESSION

Based on the latest information received from MEK sources inside Iran, including from within the Iranian regime, Tehran was caught off guard with the rapid spread of the late 2017 and early 2018 protests across the country. The regime's inherent weakness was in full display and all the control measures proved ineffective.

A major reason was the use of cyber technology by the protesters to film, distribute information, and communicate with each other and with the

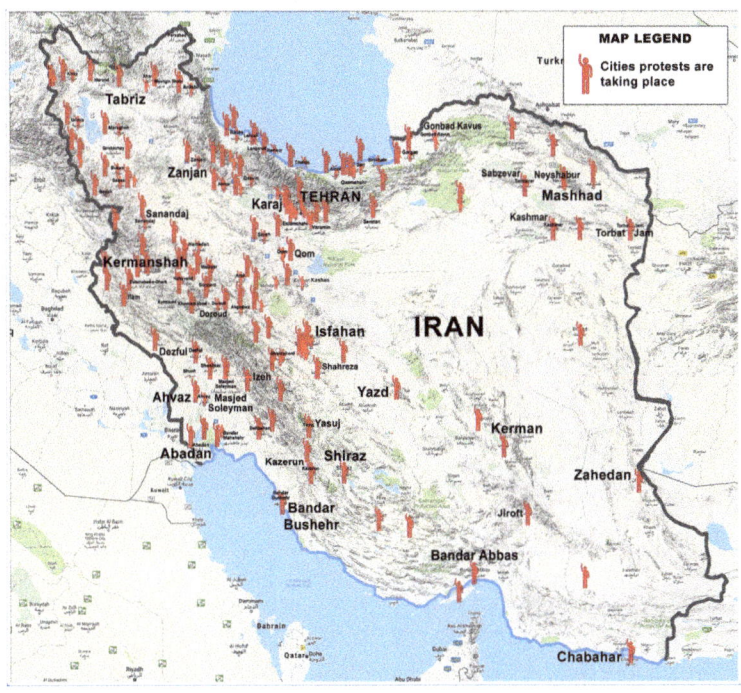

Anti-government protests sparked an uprising which expanded to 142 cities, and it continues

outside world including the western media. Some 40 million subscribers use the messaging app Telegram that accommodates secure, private and encrypted traffic to travel in and out of Iran.

On January 30, 2018, Brigadier General Gholamreza Jalali, who was appointed as the regime's Passive Defense chief by Supreme Leader Khamenei in September 2016, addressed the gathering of the provincial directors of Passive Defense. Referring to the recent nationwide protests, Jalali said, "This was a security and modern phenomenon. Its dimensions must be identified and the conspiracies must be neutralized," adding, "95 percent of our social network belongs to the Telegram app." He said that after "we shut down Telegram, … the cyber traffic reduced by 80%" then "homegrown apps gained momentum… and security forces were able to carry out timely arrests and identify the leaders" of the uprising.[20]

Borrowing from their playbook for stifling the flow of information during the 2009 uprising, within 24 hours after the uprising started on December 28th, the regime officials decided to take drastic steps to take control, cut and filter the Internet and social media platforms. The only wildcard was the secure Telegram app used by 40 million subscribers.

Mohammad-Javad Azari Jahromi, the Minister of Information and Communications Technology, worked in close collaboration with the IRGC's Intelligence organization, and its most senior official, Hossein Taeb, to take a series of extensive measures to regain control over all communications amongst the public and with the outside world. The IRGC took full control of the operations to execute these measures. The newly defined playbook included the following measures:

- Delay the access to Internet through speed limitation and

---

20. Jalali; Telegram's Cryptocurrency will affect our businesses and banks, State-run Mehr News Agency (Farsi), January 30, 2018, https://www.mehrnews.com/news/4214211/

connection throttling to cause severe slow speed and drive users away, given the cost of usage per minute.

- Cut off access to the global Internet in the affected areas where the uprising continued and spread, and then open the regime's own "Halal Internet" for full control. This measure was first tested for several hours in Tehran.

- Interrupt mobile and SMS networks in the affected areas.

- Promote the use of spyware-enabled mobile apps such as Mobogram and other apps such as Telegram Farsi, Telegram Black, Telegram Talayi, Hotgram, and Soroush.

- Station plain-clothed IRGC agents from the cyberspace coordination office of the Intelligence Organization in communication centers in Tehran for surveillance and eavesdropping on mobile communications and social networks.

- Launch an extensive cyber PSYOP and social engineering efforts to lure users away from Telegram, promote rumors about those participating in the protests, spread fake news about no protests or cancelled protests, threaten users to leave channels related to nationwide uprising, spread fake photos amongst the various uprising channels and then discredit those channel for spreading fake news.

During the second wave of protests that started on February 1, 2018, and included Tehran, Isfahan, Kermanshah, Rasht, Sanandaj, and Tuyserkan, to name a few, the IRGC used the same tactics. Reports from areas in Tehran, Isfahan, and Sanandaj indicated that Internet was slowed down significantly to prevent uploading pictures and video clips on the spot.

Students at Tehran University chanting "reformers, hardliners, the game is now over"

This Instagram user (samira.66887722) claims to be a local of 4 different Iranian cities (Bandar Abbas in the south, Gorgan in the north, Shiraz in south central, and Najafabad, in central Iran) and describing any reports of protests in those cities as a lie; a clear fake news intended to discourage protesters from joining.

samira.66887722 من خودم ساکن بندر عباس هستم . اقا اینجا هیچ خبری نیست. همه چی ارومه . چرا خبر دورغ میذاری؟؟؟؟؟؟؟

samira.66887722 من خودم ساکن گرگان هستم . اقا اینجا هیچ خبری نیست . همه چی ارومه.چرا خبر دورغ میذاری خب ؟؟؟؟؟

samira.66887722 من خودم ساکن شیراز هستم. اقا اینجا هیچ خبری نیست همه چی ارومه. چرا اخبار دورغ میذاری؟؟؟؟؟؟؟؟؟

samira.66887722 من خودم ساکن نجف اباد اصفهان هستم بابا اینجا هیچ خبری نیست. همه چی ارومه. چرا خبر دورغ میذاری؟؟؟؟؟؟؟؟؟

IRGC'S FRONT COMPANIES & APPS

CAFÉ BAZAAR

Café Bazaar is the **Iranian regime's Android mobile app marketplace** founded in February 2010 by primarily graduates and students from Sharif University of Technology in Tehran.

Café Bazaar logo

The founding members of this company are members of the paramilitary Basiji Students, which is affiliated to IRGC intelligence network and the cyber sector of Ammar Base of the IRGC Intelligence Organization. The co-founder of the *Café Bazaar* is Hessam Mir Armandehi, a computer science graduate from Sharif University of Technology. One of the developers and founders of *Café Bazaar* is Reza Mohammadi Qayeghchi.

In addition to the active and daily relationship with Ammar Cyberspace base, this site also has a direct connection with the Iranian Cyber Police (FATA).

Café Bazaar provides its services specifically to Farsi-speaking users and offers more than 25,000 downloadables in Farsi and other international apps for gaming, social media, messaging and other uses.

Like other homegrown apps, the **Café Bazaar** app, **Bazaar-7.13.2.apk,** has embedded malicious code and spyware.[21] The threat score for the app is 100/100 with 3 malicious indicators and 11 suspicious indicators including:

a. Has the ability to read SMS contents (e.g. to read verification codes)
b. Has the ability to get the wifi MAC address (may be used to fingerprint device)
c. Has the ability to read the device ID (e.g. IMEI or ESN)
d. Found an indicator for SMS sending capabilities

Cafe Bazaar co-founder Hessam Armandehi (left) with Sorena Sattari vice president for science and technology

Sorena Sattari and IRGC Brig Gen. Mohammad Baghari, Chief of Staff for the Armed Forces of the Iranian regime

21 See Hybrid Analysis at https://www.hybrid-analysis.com/sample/9cedffcd8d1632b04918a9b417b4eb1b46eb-0d543e99ef1bd705458815b19945?environmentId=200

THREAT ANALYSIS OF FAKE APPS ON *CAFÉ* BAZAAR

Since December 31, 2017, the Iranian regime has started an intense campaign promoting several leading domestic messaging services as alternatives to Telegram. There are close to 100 apps with embedded malicious code and spyware that are domestically developed and are unofficial fork versions of Telegram.

These messaging apps are found on the domestic app store **Café Bazzar** and managed by cyberwarfare actors linked to IRGC.

A user tweet: When you install Mobogram, it adds you to Hanista channel without your permission

Some of these apps are also available on **App Store**, **GitHub** and **Google Play** despite reports and user reviews warning they contain spyware embedded by the Iranian regime's app developers. The spread of these apps outside Iran will put Internet users across the world at significant risk, increasing the rate of malware infections.

A user tweet : Mobogram sends 7 GB of data while Telegram is blocked and no VPN is connected

Malware analysis of top 6 apps indicates consistent threat score of 100/100. More alarmingly, these apps have the ability to:

1. execute code after reboot
2. open an Internet connection
3. dial a phone number
4. record audio
5. read device ID (IMEI or ESN)
6. send an SMS
7. have Spyware/Information Retrieval (found on Wispi app installs a monitor for incoming SMS)
8. execute bot commands
9. access external storage
10. query the phone location (GPS)
11. find a reference to an external IP address lookup service
12. antivirus detection – check for presence
13. anti-reverse engineering to look for debuggers/analysis tools
14. embedded IP address in binary/memory with a port assignment so user's data can be sent bi-directionally

Research shows that most of the top six malicious apps armed with spyware or malware are also found on App Store, Google Play, and GitHub. They include:

Name	Café Bazaar	Appstore	GitHub	Googleplay
Mobogram	Yes	Yes	-	-
Hotgram	Yes	-	-	-
Telegram Farsi	Yes	-	Yes	-
Telegram Talayi	Yes	-		-
Wispi	Yes	Yes	-	Yes
Telegram Black	Yes	-	-	Yes

Top six malicious messaging apps

LURING MOBILE SUBSCRIBERS

Azari Jahromi advertises homegrown messaging apps

To entice subscribers to download and install these apps, they appear to offer much faster Internet connection rates, a feature appealing to users who have per minute usage plans in Iran. Additionally, these apps have a Farsi user navigation interface which makes it much easier than Telegram's non-Farsi interface for those who prefer to operate in a Farsi environment.

Due to the embedded malicious code, once used, user access to certain channels is blocked. These services also seriously compromise the user's privacy, as their traffic passes through the regime's dedicated servers for automated IRGC surveillance and monitoring (See Appendix on Wispi app).

According to MEK sources, these apps have unfettered access to the user's contacts. These apps spy on users and force them to leave Telegram channels that are deemed to be associated with the opposition or the uprising.

Some of these apps, like **Hotgram**, even have an intimidating pop up with warning messages urging users to avoid banned channels.

Dear user,
Due to complaint received about your misuse of the account, your account will Be removed. To avoid that you can:
1. Send us your Telegram contact
2. Visit the robot below and follow the Instruction to avoid deactivation of your account. @Spamtelegrammbot
If you ignore this security message, your account will be blocked for good.
Respectfully yours, Telegram Management Team

An intimidating pop up with warning message to urge users to get out of the banned channels.

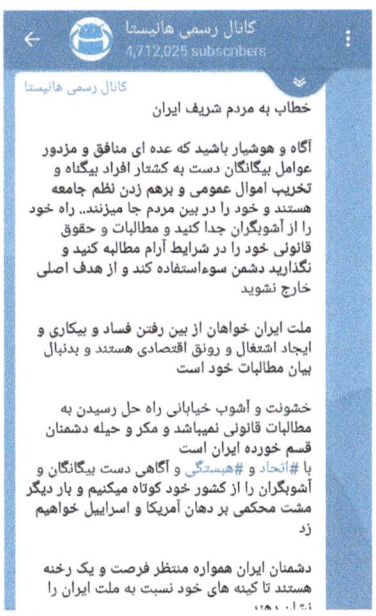

Warning messages by Official Hanista Channel to stay away from the opposition channels

COMMERCIALIZATION OF *CAFÉ* BAZAAR

Mohammad Javad Azari Jahromi, the Iranian regime's Minister of Information and Communication Technology, is a key player in the new enterprise of promoting and disseminating homegrown apps and services, incentivizing the public to gain better, faster and cheaper access if they leverage these services.

On January 22, 2018, the state-run ILNA news agency reported an official meeting of Rouhani's Deputy for Science and Technology, Sorena Satari, with the leaders of *Café Bazaar* expressing the importance of such "large and important" start-up plans in Iran.[22] During this visit, Hessam Mir Armandehi, the co-founder of *Café Bazaar*, announced an Amsterdam-

---

[22] "Presidential deputy in science and technology affairs visits Hezardastan Holding," state-run ILNA, January 22, 2018. (Translated from Farsi), goo.gl/oFC8Y8

based business International Internet Investment Coöperatief (IIC) is planning to invest in *Café Bazaar*. Armandehi added, "The money will be used to develop new services including a cloud service."[23]

It is deeply troubling to see how a front company related to the IRGC intelligence network and the cyber sector of Ammar Base of the IRGC intelligence organization has rebranded itself as a "tech start-up" and is seeking funding from a Dutch company. Moreover, there is no doubt that the Iranian regime is currently hard at work to test the success of these apps on the people of Iran first. If not confronted, its next victims will be the people of other countries. These apps have embedded malware, they are written in other languages and are available beyond the regime's own app market place, *Café Bazaar*. The current digital crackdown on Iran's protesters and people could affect almost anyone who has been in contact with them, because of such elevated internal cyberwarfare techniques and tactics through mobile apps and messaging platforms.

HANISTA PROGRAMING GROUP

Hanista is an IRGC front company, introduced as a programing group. It is led and managed by IRGC and IRGC Intelligence organization. Its website claims that it was formed in 2014 and it focuses on enabling Iran's cyber commerce with mobile apps, in Farsi language, and within the regime's-controlled Internet environment.

23."Dutch Company to Invest in Iran Technology Firm," Financial Tribune, January 24, 2018, https://financialtribune.com/articles/ sci-tech/80615/dutch-company-to-invest-in-iran-technology-firm

The group developed and owns the **Mobogram** app, and as mentioned, the app is the latest product in the IRGC's surveillance arsenal to advance the new wave of cyberwarfare.

More than 8,000 people have been arrested since the uprising started in late December 2017. The MEK has obtained information from some of those who have been interrogated by the MOIS in recent weeks, who have said that upon their release, the IRGC assigned a "surveillance officer" for each released protester and ordered them "to leave the Telegram environment and enter the controlled environment of Mobogram."

All the Telegram channel administrators, subscribers and members of social groups who have gone through this process with IRGC and MOIS continue to receive calls and inquiries from the regime to identify others.

Because these apps are associated with a telephone number and are forks of the original Telegram, once the user leaves Telegram and starts using Mobogram, all their contacts in the original Telegram app are automatically exposed to IRGC's surveillance. Forced befriending and adding of IRGC members to the existing channels to monitor messages and new users is also used to expand surveillance programs.

WHAT IS MOBOGRAM AND HOW DOES IT WORK?

Mobogram is an unofficial Farsi version of the original Telegram. Based on the information received by MEK sources inside Iran, Mobogram was developed under the supervision of the IRGC and the IRGC Intelligence organization. The use of Mobogram as a mobile endpoint agent for identification of protesters was first tested earlier in 2017.

Since the Iranian regime's request to spy on subscribers was rejected by Telegram, the IRGC has invested significantly in the development of its own

Pavel Durov on his tweet disclosed that Iran's ministry of ICT had asked him to provide them with spying and censorship

app, Mobogram, whose embedded spyware and surveillance features can trigger significant access and authority without the user's consent and awareness.

The IRGC uses the malicious features embedded in Mobogram to spy, identify, threaten and eventually arrest protesters who used Mobogram during the uprising. The malicious codes embedded in Mobogram are undetected and unnoticed by the mobile user. If Mobogram is installed by an administrator of a Telegram channel on his/her phone, the malicious code allows the IRGC to gain full access to the entire list of that channel's subscribers.

Threat analysis of Mobogram reveals a score of 100/100 with 3 malicious indicators (i.e., Has the ability to execute code after reboot) and 5 suspicious indicators (i.e., Has the ability to record audio).[24] Regrettably, despite user reviews complaining about embedded spyware in this app, Mobogram continues to be available on App Store. The name identified with

24. See Hybrid Analysis at https://www.hybrid-analysis.com/sample/ 1a022c116bc390f7752b6d5d3971dfec-c5ea382d05c50da19ec7866bd0aa4199?environmentId=200

Mobogram in App Store is Babak Aghakhani.[25]

The Mobogram download page on *Café Bazaar* shows more than one million active installs.[26]

The Telegram channel of Hanista, the developer of Mobogram, has more than 4.7 million subscribers. Based on testing of the app, upon installing, Mobogram forces users to become subscribers of the Hanista Channel. Therefore, Mobogram's subscribers can potentially be similar to those subscribed to the Hanista Channel.

A Case of the IRGC's use of Mobogram to run surveillance and launch arrests:

On March 15, 2017, the regime arrested 12 administrators of so-called "pro-reformist" Telegram channels.[27] Seyyed Hossein Naghavi Hosseini, a spokesman for the National Security and Policy Committee of the regime's Parliament, was quoted by the state-run media as falsely suggesting that the arrests were carried out with the help of Telegram and through the Telegram server. However, this was not the case. In fact, Telegram rejected the regime's demands to cooperate, per a statement by its CEO.[28]

The arrest of the 12 Telegram channels' administrators was carried out by spying on 2 admins who installed Mobogram app on their phones. The IRGC was able to identify the rest of the admins using people who were active on Mobogram and later arrested.

---

25. Babak Aghakhani is an online identity and has not been authenticated.
26. Mobogram page on Café Bazaar, https://cafebazaar.ir/app/com.hanista.mobogram/?l=en
27. "Admins of 12 Reformist Telegram Channels Arrested in Iran Ahead of May 2017 Election," Center for Human Rights in Iran, March 21, 2017, https://www.iranhumanrights.org/2017/03/12-reformist-telegram-channel-admins-arrested/
28. See the CEO's tweet: "Iranian ministry of ICT demanded that @telegram provided them with spying and censorship tools. We ignored the demand, they blocked us." October 20, 2015, https://twitter.com/durov/status/656551981226528768

HOW THE REGIME USES HOMEGROWN APPS TO REPRESS ITS PEOPLE

IRGC
The Islamic Revolutionary Guard Corps works with the Ministry of Intelligence to create smartphone applications used for surveillance and repression.

HANISTA
Hanista is an IRGC front company, introduced as a programming group, which focuses on enabling Iran's cyber commerce with mobile apps in Farsi language.

MOBOGRAM
Mobogram, an app developed by Hanista, is presented by the regime as an alternative to Telegram. Its "controlled environment" lets the regime surveil users, identify and arrest protestors.

Café Bazaar
The homegrown market place, modeled after Google Play, is supervised by the IRGC.

cafebazaar.ir

App Store
Mobogram is available on App Store, a digital istribution platform, by Apple Inc., for mobile apps on its iOS operating system.

WHO IS AT RISK?

The Iranian regime's cyberwarfare is now targeting individual mobile users through spyware and malicious surveillance code that can record

Telegram API Terms of Service

We welcome all developers to use our API and source code to create Telegram-like messaging applications on our platform free of charge. In order to ensure consistency and security across the Telegram ecosystem, all third-party client apps must comply with the following Terms of Service.

1. Privacy & Security

1.1. Telegram is a privacy-oriented platform. All client apps must, therefore, guard their users' privacy with utmost care and comply with our Security Guidelines.
1.2. Developers are welcome to add new features or improve and extend existing Telegram features provided that these modifications do not violate these Terms of Service.
1.3. As a client developer, you must make sure that all the basic features of the main Telegram apps function correctly and in an expected way both in your app and when users of your app communicate with other Telegram users. It is forbidden to force users of other Telegram clients to download your app in order to view certain messages and content sent using your app.
1.4. It is forbidden to interfere with the basic functionality of Telegram. This includes but is not limited to: making actions on behalf of the user without the user's knowledge and consent, preventing self-destructing content from disappearing, preventing last seen and online statuses from being displayed correctly, tampering with the 'read' statuses of messages (e.g. implementing a 'ghost mode'), preventing typing statuses from being sent/displayed, etc.

2. Transparency

2.1. You must obtain your own api_id for your application.
2.2. We offer our API free of charge, but your users must be aware of the fact that your app uses the Telegram API and is part of the Telegram ecosystem. This fact must be featured prominently in the app's description in the app stores and in the in-app intro if your app has it.
2.3. To avoid confusion, the title of your app must not include the word "Telegram". An exception can be made if the word "Telegram" is preceded with the word "Unofficial" in the title.
2.4. You must not use the official Telegram logo for your app. Both the Telegram brand and its logo are registered trademarks protected by law in almost every country.

3. Advertising & Monetization

3.1. Developers are allowed to monetize their coding efforts through advertising or other legitimate means.
3.2. If you decide to monetize your app, you must clearly mention all the methods of monetization that are used in your app in all its app store descriptions.

4. Breach of terms

4.1. If your app violates these terms, we will notify the Telegram account responsible for the app about the breach of terms.
4.2. If you do not update the app to fix the highlighted issues within 10 days, we will have to discontinue your access to Telegram API and contact the app stores about the removal of your apps that are using the Telegram API in violation of these terms.

We reserve the right to expand these terms and guidelines as the need arises. We will inform client developers of such changes via an in-app notification to their accounts connected to the app in question.

Telegram API terms of service

audio, SMS and read device IDs without the user's knowledge or consent. Millions of mobile users in Iran are victims today and millions more will be victims elsewhere if the Iranian regime's latest cyberwarfare is not confronted with effective countermeasures.

It is highly suspicious why the Iranian regime, which is hell-bent on controlling the Internet inside Iran, would make these apps available to other mobile users around the world through App Store, Google Play, and GitHub. Most of these apps piggyback on either the names, designs or functions of Telegram popular apps in an attempt to trick the Iranian people into downloading them. Some (i.e., Wispi) are available in other languages as well.[29] While many of them have negative reviews and complaints about the apps being infected, they continue to be available for download on popular app stores. The dissemination of these apps outside of Iran will enable the IRGC to spy globally and at will. The intrusive nature of these apps, and their embedded malicious code and surveillance capabilities, are in violation of Telegram's published API Term of Service.

These apps play a direct role in the regime's cyber repression and empower the IRGC and the IRGC Intelligence organization in their ongoing human rights violations against the Iranian people. The existence of some of these apps on Github, Google Play and App Store is in violation of Executive Order 13606. The Order clearly prevents any entity, whether in Iran or elsewhere, to facilitate the Iranian regime in its "computer and network disruption, monitoring, and tracking" and "or otherwise provided, directly or indirectly, goods, services, or technology" that can be used to "enable serious human rights abuses by or on behalf of the Government of Iran."[30]

---

29. See the appendix for more specific details and deeper analysis on Wispi.

30. "Executive Order 13606—Blocking the Property and Suspending Entry into the United States of Certain Persons With Respect to Grave Human Rights Abuses by the Governments of Iran and Syria Via Information Technology," The American Presidency Project, April 22, 2012, http://www.presidency.ucsb.edu/ws/index.php?pid=100679

Given the political dynamics on the ground, the cyber conflict between the Iranian people and the regime will continue to escalate since protests have become more routine and widespread. There is threat intelligence available from industry and law enforcement that can be used to raise awareness and foster proactive defense measures against the IRGC's cyberwarfare activities. There is an ongoing security awareness campaign amongst the Iranian citizens to evade surveillance, avoid the IRGC's apps, and recognize phishing or insider threats amongst various online communities and groups.

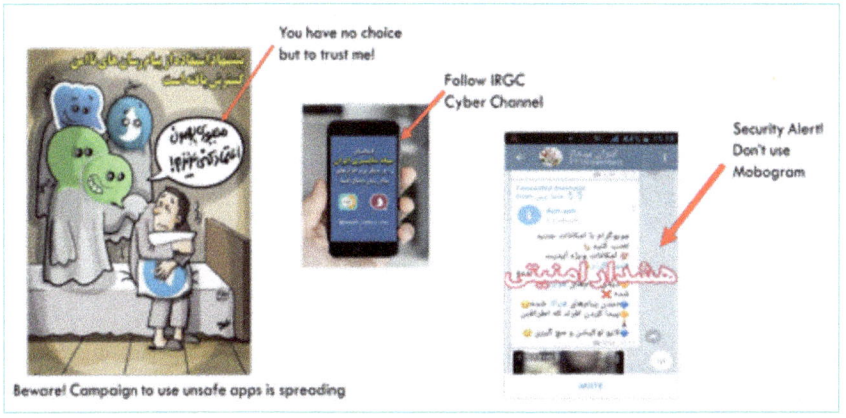

IRGC cyberwarfare campaign to intimidate Telegram users and force them to use homegrown apps

KEY PLAYERS IN IRAN'S LATEST CYBERWARFARE

The regime's cyberwarfare is primarily led by the IRGC. The Ministry of Intelligence (MOIS), and the State Security Forces (NAJA) also have cyberwarfare sections.

The IRGC's central headquarters for cyberwarfare is known as the Ammar Cyberspace Base.

IRGC's cyberwarfare organization is under the command of the IRGC's Intelligence Organization, which is headed by the cleric Hossein Taeb and his deputy, Brigadier-general Hossein Nejat.

The IRGC's Cyberspace Base includes a 15-member assembly. Some of them are:

1. Hojjat ol-Islam Alireza Panahian, *Head of Supreme Leader Ali Khamenei's "think tank for universities."*

2. Hojjat ol-Islam Mehdi Taeb, *Seminary and University Professor*

3. Saeed Qasemi, *Director of the Cultural Institute of the Misagh*

4. Hojjat ol-Islam Mohammad Mehdi Mandegari, *Chairman of the Board of the Cultural Institute of the Martyrs Sire*

5. Nader Talebzadeh, *Author, director, and presenter of the Raz program. He was also on the board of directors of Popular Front of Islamic Revolution Forces-JAMNA*

6. Hassan Abbasi, *Chairman of the Security Doctrine Without Borders*

7. Mohammad Hossein Rostami, *Director of Ammar's Cyberspace Base site, Amaryoon*

The following organizational charts were compiled by the MEK's network inside Iran, which demonstrates the new organizational alignment for the current wave of cyber repressions led by the IRGC.

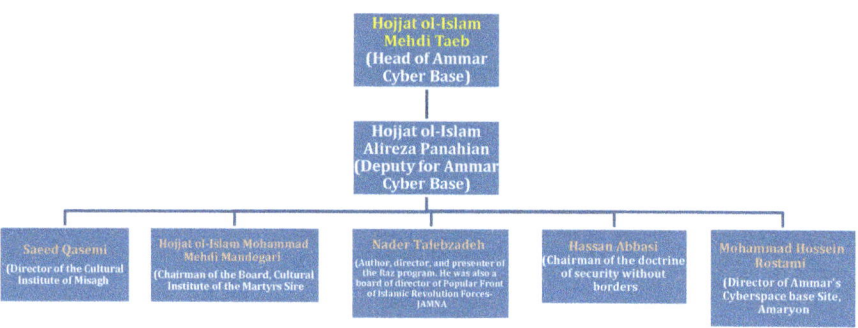

Ammar Cyberspace base organizational chart

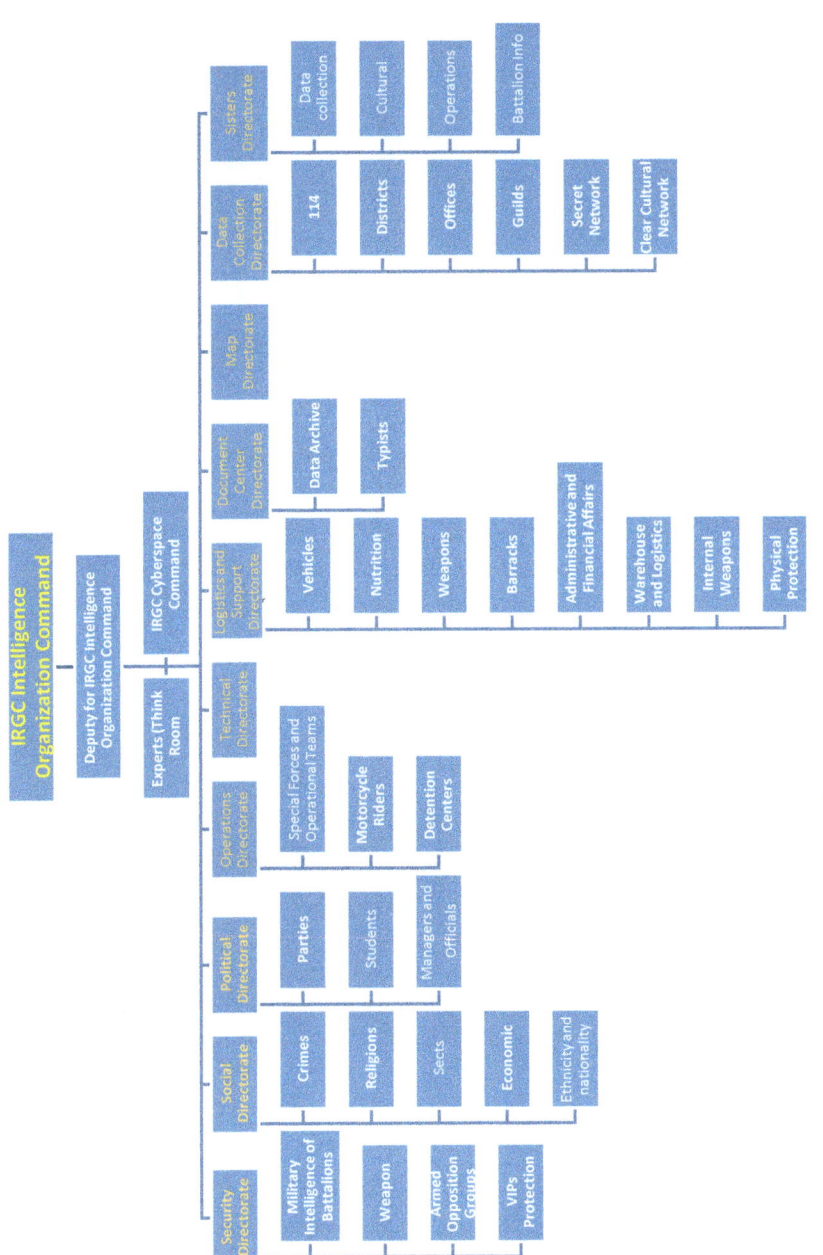

The IRGC Intelligence organization chart

THE KEY PLAYER

Beyond Iran's supreme leader and president, there is one person who brings together the technical coordination and logistical efforts for cyber repression. This individual is Mohammad Javad Azari Jahromi, Minister of Information and Communication Technology.

Azari Jahromi, the regime's minster of Information and Communication Technology

Jahromi worked for Iran's notorious Intelligence Ministry for several years and has been accused of interrogating those arrested during the 2009 uprising. He is an engineer by education and intelligence officer by profession. Jahromi is intimately involved and engaged in the design and deployment of Iran's surveillance infrastructure which has enabled the regime to use preventive methods for DNS Redirect, Broadband speed limitations, filtering of blacklisted URL's, hosts and keywords, and enhancement of Content Control software acquired from the West. Additionally, he has worked hard to influence key ISP's in Iran to utilize interceptive methods such as Man in the Middle, Deep Packet Inspection or Traffic Analysis. Jahromi has also coordinated efforts among the closed loop of connectivity through reactive methods which entails Periodic Blocking of SSL, responding to patterns of users' behavior, connection throttling, identifying users and informing MOIS leading to arrests.

While Jahromi downplays his former role at the Intelligence Ministry, on August 20, 2017, Rouhani told the regime's parliament "Mr. Jahromi attended the meetings of the Supreme Council of Cyberspace for a while on behalf of Mr. Alavi (Minister of Intelligence), when he was in the

Ministry of Intelligence. The reason I insisted that he join [the cabinet] was because we have a lot of complicated issues in security matters. If I am not in a meeting, one must be there who knows the security [field].[31]"
In an interview with Tasnim News (Quds force news agency), Jahromi said that he "is proud to work in the Ministry of Intelligence."[32]

Jahromi is committed to Khamenei's cyberwarfare agenda and is on the record for saying: "Our doctrine in the field of cyberspace is only one doctrine, and it is the doctrine of the Supreme Leader [Khamenei], who has said that the threat of cyberspace is to the extent that it has become a killing field for the youth."[33] In his own words, he is committed to "cleanse and clean our [Iran's] cyberspace."[34]

Jahromi was the key player behind the blocking of messaging platform, Telegram, on December 31, 2017. While Telegram was unblocked a few days later, his new tactics, in coordination with the IRGC, is to impose connection throttling and speed limitations on Telegram traffics. The Iranian regime hopes the slow performance will drive users away from using the official Telegram mobile app.

---

31. "President at the Majlis session for vote of confidence for proposed cabinet members," state-run Iran daily, August 21, 2017. s(Translated from Farsi), http://www.magiran.com/npview.asp?ID=3613884
32. "Azari Jahromi: I am proud to have been an intelligence agent," state-affiliated Tasnim news agency, August 29, 2017 (Translated from Farsi), https://www.tasnimnews.com/fa/news/1396/06/07/1505035/
33. "Our policy is not to shut down cyberspace, but we are not weak against it," state-run 33 Tasnim news agency, August 15, 2017 (Translated from Farsi), https://www.tasnimnews.com/fa/news/1396/05/24/1492849/
34. Ibid.

POLICY RECOMMENDATIONS: COUNTERMEASURES TO CYBER REPRESSION IN IRAN

What gives confidence to the Iranian regime to continue cyber repression is the international community's inaction and ambivalence. As such, the European Union and the United States have added responsibility to act.

- Cyber repression by the Iranian regime must not be analyzed in a vacuum and separate from other repressive measure at home, export of terrorism and nuclear expansion. For this reason, in order to counter Tehran's increasing cyber threats, a comprehensive and decisive policy must be adopted. Such a policy should include the full implementation of the current sanctions against the Islamic Revolutionary Guard Corps (IRGC) and its front companies, as well as imposing sanctions that would deprive the regime access to the international banking and financial systems. All measures necessary to evict the IRGC from the regional countries, especially Syria, must also be undertaken.

- All persons and institutions involved in cyberwarfare must be subjected to tough sanctions and denied access to the international market.

- While the clerical regime is denying the Iranian people access to Internet and the free flow of information, its massive propaganda machine, especially the state radio and television continue to spread false and misleading information. Iran's propaganda machine is part and parcel of its machinery of suppression. It must be subjected to comprehensive sanctions.

- The Iranian people need safe, secure, and free access to Internet. Additional circumvention tools are needed and should be offered as free services to the Iranians. These solutions should be scaled up to handle the traffic of millions of Iranian evading the regime's surveillance, so that the Iranian people and protesters can continue to have unimpeded access to the global Internet service for the ongoing cyber resistance in Iran.

- Making apps and tools available in Farsi language will be a tremendous assistance that tech companies can provide to the people of Iran.

- Enforce security hygiene and measures in app market places. Prevent the proliferation of spyware-enabled apps by the Iranian regime, particularly those related to the IRGC. Remove all such known apps from the Internet.

- Enforce the Executive Order 13606 which clearly prohibits any entity to facilitate the Iranian regime in its "computer and network disruption, monitoring, and tracking" and "or otherwise provided, directly or indirectly, goods, services, or technology" that can be used to "enable serious human rights abuses by or on behalf of the Government of Iran," and urge other western countries to do the same in preventing the Iranian regime's cyber repression.

APPENDIX

DEEPER ANALYSIS OF WISPI APPS
HACKERS JOIN FAKE APP MARKET

DEEPER ANALYSIS OF WISPI APPS

Wispi is another mobile app with very peculiar on-line information. According to description on line, Wispi is developed by SG Atlantic Limited. SG Atlantic Limited has a website which has not been updated since 2015. The app is available in other languages. The company is based in Hong Kong, according to the website info. The website has limited information about the nature of the company and there are no specific names associated with the company or the app developers.

What is interesting about this that no matter if Chinese or the regime developed it, majority of its users are in Iran and it is a malicious app with embedded features that direct traffics only to Iran's main ISP, Shatel.

According to web traffic analysis by Alexa, 95.2% of Wispiapp.com traffic is from Iran. Wispi app is available on Googleplay, and Appstore. The app was last updated on Jan 5, 2018. According to the published description of the app on Googleplay:

> Get Wispi and connect to the world freely!
>
> Wispi is a free messaging and calling app that connects you with your friends around the world. You may even call or message friends who do not have access to the internet!
>
> - Free voice and video calls
> - Private and group chat
> - Channels - Broadcast yourself with unlimited followers or follow
> - your favorite broadcaster
> - Call any phone number (landline or mobile) either free or at low cost
> - Send SMS to anyone in the world
> - Find new friends near you using location-based search, Wispi PIN, and recommendations
> - View, listen and share YouTube videos and iTunes music
> - Social – Browse through attractive content and channels
> - Awesome stickers, animations, hilarious audio effects and much more
>
> Now available in 13 languages:
> Arabic, Bahasa Indonesia, English, French, Japanese, Korean, Persian (Farsi), Portuguese, Spanish, Thai, Traditional & Simplified Chinese, and Vietnamese.
>
> Developer
> Visit websiteEmail hi@wispiapp.comPrivacy Policy
> AIA Central, 1 Connaught Rd Central, Central, Hong Kong

Wispi app features

Using packet capture tools, one can see that all the traffic coming and going from mobile device are only connecting to certain IP addresses that belong to one of the largest ISPs in Iran, Shatel.[35]

---

35. 185.73.2.15 - Iran - SHATEL Network - IP address location and data (https://db-ip.com/185.73.2.15)

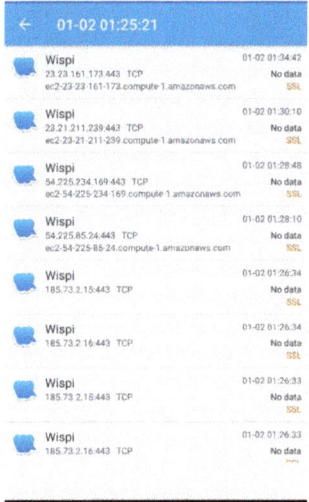

Packet capture here is an example where the Wispi app communicates to 185.73.2.15 and 185.73.2.16. According to db-ip.com, the IP block 185.73.2 belongs to one of Iran's largest ISP - SHATEL Network – an IPv4 address owned by SHATEL Network and located in Tehran (District 3), Iran.

Threat analysis of Wispi Mobile App: Malware analysis of Wispi shows a threat score of 100/100 with 3 malicious indicators (i.e., Installs a monitor for incoming SMS) and 8 suspicious indicators (i.e., Found an IP/URL artifact that was identified as malicious by at least one reputation engine).[36]

About Shatel: Established in 2002 and its services cover "the whole country and takes the largest share of Internet customers market and additional services, particularly in the field of high speed Internet ADSL2+."[37]

ISP Name	Website	Linkedin	Key personnel
Shatel	http://en.shatel.ir/	https://www.linkedin.com/company/2274800/	Ahmad Nakhjavani(CEO) Mina Deljou(VP of Sales and Marketing) Farhad Karamzadeh(CPO) Hossein Shanehsaz zadeh(Vice Chairman) Farhad Soltani (CTO)

Shatel ISP info

36. See Hybrid Analysis, https://www.hybrid-analysis.com/sample/6deb4b526376f658b6142cc73d-2ba86339354690e08b428a960a0429e01536cb?environmentId=200
37. See the Shatel website, http://en.shatel.ir/

TELEGRAM FARSI

With looking at Telegram Farsi, one can see how a hacker has turned into developer of a fake app at the service of the Iranian regime. The hacker's fake online identity is Mohammad Reza Mokhtarabadi. He has identified himself with PersianFox engaged in defacing of websites since 2005, according to zone-h.org reports.[38] PersianFox has been active under the domain persianfox.ir. Looking through the web archive related to persianfox.ir, one can see how the fake name Mohammad Reza Mokhtarabadi has been active in hacking websites around the world and teaching others how to develop malware.

In 2016, the site persianfox.ir was removed. The same group (Persian Fox), showed up on app market places offering Telegram Farsi. This fake Telegram application (PersianFox messenger) is available on *Café Bazaar* with more than 2 millions download. Mohammad Reza Mokhtarabadi name also appears on GitHub promoting his mobile app Telegram Farsi.

Like other apps, Telegram Farsi threat score is 100/100 with 5 malicious indicators and 10 suspicious indicators. The app has the ability to query the phone location (GPS), the ability to read the device ID (e.g. IMEI or ESN), and possibly checks for the presence of an Antivirus engine.[39]

ABOUT PERSIANFOX

Since 2005, the hacker community has seen activities by a group called PersianFox. According to zone-h.org PersianFox is known for its hacking activities, particularly, focusing on Mass defacement, Re-defacement, Home–defacement. Looking through web archive, Mohammad Reza

---

38. See, Zone-h.org, http://www.zone-h.org/archive/notifier=Persian%20Fox/page=29
39. See Hybrid Analysis, https://www.hybrid-analysis.com/sample/e6bd6ebcf080ba7664cf4635b5749cfa6cdae-c42f5ab9e341cd164a86a9ffe69?environmentId=200

Mokhtarabadi is the pseudo-name associated with PersianFox. His website PersianFox was originally listed under perdianfox.ir.

Self-reporting of a few websites he hacked in Canada on October 12, 2010.[40]

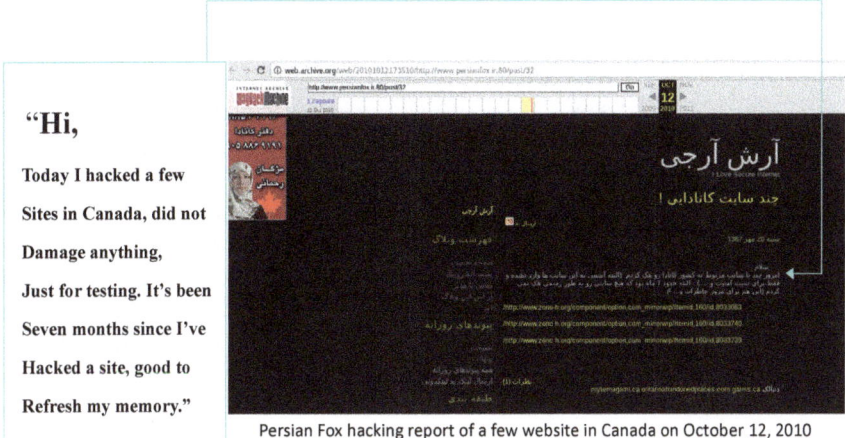

"Hi,

Today I hacked a few Sites in Canada, did not Damage anything, Just for testing. It's been Seven months since I've Hacked a site, good to Refresh my memory."

Persian Fox hacking report of a few website in Canada on October 12, 2010

In March of 2013, Persian Fox website (persianfox.ir) rebranded itself as a social media tool developing site:[41]

Mohammad Reza Mokhtarabadi giving his email in an article and asking people to contact him if they want him to sell them an application for running their own social media website like Facebook.

Persian Fox website (persianfox.ir) rebranded itself as a social media tool developing site

---

40. See Web archive: http://web.archive.org/web/20101013045722/http://www.zone-h.org/mirror/id/8033083, the day before this report, he posted another evidence of hacking on zone-h.org referring to himself as PersianFox security group

41. See document saved on Web Archive, http://web.archive.org/web/20130323234412/http://persianfox.ir/

Persian Fox website (persianfox.ir) showed on August 22, 2013 that Mohammad Reza began recruiting online:[42]

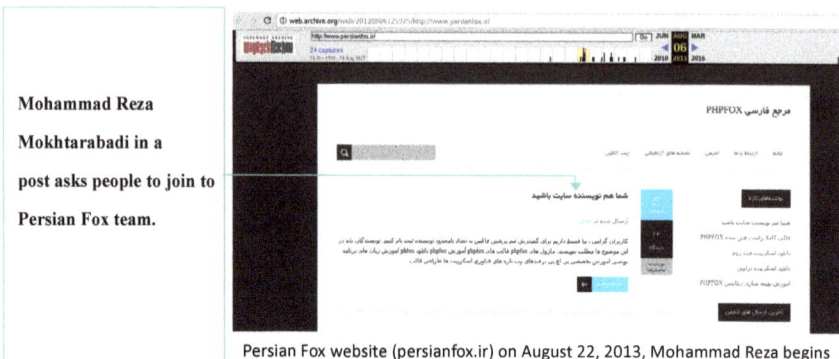

Mohammad Reza Mokhtarabadi in a post asks people to join to Persian Fox team.

Persian Fox website (persianfox.ir) on August 22, 2013, Mohammad Reza begins recruiting online

On March 31, 2014, Mohammad Reza published his bio and Facebook profile on persianfox.ir site, clearly fabricating his online identity age as an 18-year-old student, yet he has a profile of being an active hacker on zone-h.org since 2005:[43]

I am Mohammad Reza, 18-year-old, student, and have a lot of interest in writing code, especially web authoring. Since there really aren't many sites in Farsi that focus on starting a social site, I decided to start this site myself. Contact me: mmokhtarabadi@gmail.com

Mohammad Reza publishes his bio and Facebook profile on persianfox.ir site, clearly fabricating his online identity age as an 18-year-old student

---

42. See document saved on Web Archive, http://web.archive.org/web/20130806125925/http://www.persianfox.ir/

43. See Web Archive document: http://web.archive.org/web/20140331075035/http://persianfox.ir/

On August 3, 2015, Persianfox.ir promoted training on malware development:[44]

Persianfox.ir promotes training on malware development

On August 19, 2015, **PersianFox website (persianfox.ir)** moved to a new level on Facebook, going from a group to communities:[45]

Persian Fox website (persianfox.ir) moves from to a new level on Facebook from a group to communities

44. See Web Archive document: http://web.archive.org/web/20150803090348/http://persianfox.ir:80/threads/

45. See document at Web Archive: http://web.archive.org/web/20150820095544/http://persianfox.ir/

GLOSSARY OF TERMS

Admin: channel administrator for mobile applications such as Telegram. Larger communities that need administration for inviting new members and change the group's name, send group messages, videos and photo. It is often referred to admins or administrator.

API (Application programming interface): a set of subroutine definitions, protocols, and tools for building application software. Telegram API allows building customized Telegram clients.

App marketplace: a type of digital distribution platform for computer software, often in a mobile context.

Channel: Telegram channel are a tool for broadcasting *public* messages to large audiences. In fact, a channel can have an unlimited number of subscribers.

Connection throttling: intentional slowing or speeding of an Internet service by an Internet service provider (ISP). Throttling can be used to actively limit a user's upload and download rates on programs such as video streaming.

Cyber PSYOP: the cyber psychological operation that aim to directly attack and influence the attitudes and behaviors of online and mobile users as well as the general population.

Cyber repression: repressive state sponsored measures to limit or monitor the public's access and activities online.

Cyber resistance: refers to a cyber security essential practices, including security awareness into strategic assets to enable and maintain resiliency to remain active on Internet safely, securely and with protection of privacy.

Cyberwarfare: motivated cyber-attacks targeting computers, users and networks in a deliberate and directed manner. In Iran's case, it involves both offensive and defensive operations pertaining to IRGC's focus domestically and globally.

Data alteration: unauthorized modifications to code or data, attacking its integrity. These attacks can take many different forms and have a variety of consequences.

Deep packet inspection: DPI is a complete packet inspection and information extraction (IX) is a form of computer network packet filtering that examines the data part (and possibly also the header) of a packet as it passes an inspection point (i.e., defined by IRGC requirements), searching for protocol non-compliance, viruses, spam, intrusions, or defined criteria to decide whether the packet may pass or if it needs to be routed to a different destination.

Domestic mobile apps: set of mobile apps that are developed in Iran and specifically for use on small, wireless computing devices, such as smartphones and tablets, rather than desktop or laptop computers.

Embedded malicious code: malicious software that refers to a variety of forms of harmful or intrusive software, including computer viruses, worms, Trojan horses, ransomware, spyware, adware, scareware, and other malicious programs.

Endpoint: the model around end user devices such as PCs, laptops and mobile phones.

Fingerprint device: fingerprints can be used to fully or partially identify individual users or devices even when cookies are turned off.

Forked App: aka fake apps, are mobile apps that have used Telegram open source without prior permission or adherence to API Term of Service.

Insider threat: a user from IRGC and MOIS who have gained membership status to a channel to actively monitor the inside information concerning the users' information, activities and plans.

Malware: an umbrella term used to refer to a variety of forms of malicious software, harmful or intrusive software, including computer viruses, worms, Trojan horses, ransomware, spyware, adware, scareware, and other malicious programs.

Messaging platform: a unique tools and features of apps that enables Internet users to exchange messages for individual or group communications.

Social engineering: use of human-to-human cyber interaction and gain trust in order get the user to divulge sensitive information.

Speed limitation: intentional imposition of limit to Internet access speed by imposing what are known as speed caps.

Stateful endpoint: a new terminology to explain how IRGC's access to mobile device operates with full tracking of all interaction of these devices.

Spyware: software that aims to gather information about a person or organization without their knowledge that may send such information to another entity without the user's consent.

Telegram Channel: a tool for broadcasting public messages to large audiences in Telegram. In fact, a channel can have an unlimited number of subscribers.

ABOUT NCRI-US

National Council of Resistance of Iran-US Representative Office acts as the Washington office for Iran's Parliament-in-exile, which is dedicated to the establishment of a democratic, secular, non-nuclear republic in Iran.

NCRI-US, registered as a non-profit tax-exempt organization, has been instrumental in exposing the nuclear weapons program of Iran, including the sites in Natanz, and Arak, the biological and chemical weapons program of Iran, as well as its ambitious ballistic missile program.

NCRI-US has also exposed the terrorist network of the Iranian regime, including its involvement in the bombing of Khobar Towers in Saudi Arabia, the Jewish Community Center in Argentina, its fueling of sectarian violence in Iraq and Syria, and its malign activities in other parts of the Middle East.

Our office has provided information on the human rights violations in Iran, extensive anti-government demonstrations, and the movement for democratic change in Iran.

VISIT OUR WEBSITE AT WWW.NCRIUS.ORG

YOU MAY FOLLOW US ON

@NCRIUS   NCRIUS   NCRIUS

LIST OF PUBLICATIONS
BY THE NATIONAL COUNCIL OF RESISTANCE OF IRAN, U.S.REPRESENTATIVE OFFICE

IRAN: WHERE MASS MURDERERS RULE; THE 1988 MASSACRE OF 30,000 POLITICAL PRISONERS AND THE CONTINUING ATROCITIES

DECEMBER 2017,

138 PAGES

This book is an exposé of the track record of current rulers of Iran in human rights violations. It details how 30,000 political prisoners fell victim to politicide during the summer of 1988 and showcases the most egregious political extinction of a group of people. The publication includes details about how the massacre arose, and how the perpetrators are presently engaging in the justification or cover up of the massacre.

Iran's Nuclear Core: Uninspected Military Sites, Vital to the Nuclear Weapons Program

October 2017, 52 pages

This book details how the nuclear weapons program is at the heart, and not in parallel, to the civil nuclear program of Iran. The program has been run by the Islamic Revolutionary Guards Corp (IRGC) since the beginning, and the main nuclear sites and nuclear research facilities have been hidden from the eyes of the United Nations nuclear watchdog.

Terrorist Training Camps in Iran: How Islamic Revolutionary Guards Corps Trains Foreign Fighters to Export Terrorism

June 1017, 56 pages

The book details how Islamic Revolutionary Guards Corps trains foreign fighters in 15 various camps in Iran to export terrorism. The IRGC has created a large directorate within its extraterritorial arm, the Quds Force, in order to expand its training of foreign mercenaries as part of the strategy to step up its meddling abroad in Syria, Iraq, Yemen, Bahrain, Afghanistan and elsewhere.

How Iran Regime Cheated the World: Tehran's Systematic Efforts to Cover Up its Nuclear Weapons Program

June 2014, 50 pages

This book deals with one of the most fundamental challenges that goes to the heart of the dispute regarding the Iranian regime's controversial nuclear program: to ascertain with certainty that Tehran will not pursue a nuclear bomb. Such an assurance can only be obtained through specific steps taken by Tehran in response to the international community's concerns. The monograph discusses the Iranian regime's report card as far as it relates to being transparent when addressing the international community's concerns about the true nature and the ultimate purpose of its nuclear program.

Presidential Elections in Iran: Changing Faces; Status Quo Policies

May 2017, 78 pages

The book, reviews the past 11 presidential elections, demonstrating that the only criterion for qualifying as a candidate is practical and heartfelt allegiance to the Supreme Leader. An unelected vetting watchdog, the Guardian Council makes that determination.

The Rise of Iran's Revolutionary Guards' Financial Empire: How the Supreme Leader and the IRGC Rob the People to Fund International Terror

March 2017, 174 pages

This manuscript examines some vital factors and trends, including the overwhelming and accelerating influence (especially since 2005) of the Supreme Leader and the Islamic Revolutionary Guard Corps (IRGC). This study shows how ownership of property in various spheres of the economy is gradually shifted from the population writ large towards a minority ruling elite comprised of the Supreme Leader's office and the IRGC, using 14 powerhouses, and how the money ends up funding terrorism worldwide.

How Iran Fuels Syria War: Details of the IRGC Command HQ and Key Officers in Syria

November 2016, 74 pages

This book examines how the Iranian regime has effectively engaged in the military occupation of Syria by marshaling 70,000 forces, including the Islamic Revolutionary Guard Corps (IRGC) and mercenaries from other countries into Syria; is paying monthly salaries to over 250,000 militias and agents to prolong the conflict; divided the country into 5 zones of conflict and establishing 18 command, logistics and operations centers.

Nowruz 2016 with the Iranian Resistance: Hoping for a New Day, Freedom and Democracy in Iran

April 2016, 36 pages

This book describes Iranian New Year, Nowruz celebrations at the Washington office of Iran's parliament-in-exile, the National Council of Resistance of Iran. The yearly event marks the beginning of spring. It includes select speeches by dignitaries who have attended the NCRIUS Nowruz celebrations. This book also discusses the very rich culture and the traditions associated with Nowruz for centuries.

The 2016 Vote in Iran's Theocracy: An analysis of Parliamentary & Assembly of Experts Elections

February 2016, 70 pages

This book examines all the relevant data about the 2016 Assembly of Experts as well as Parliamentary elections ahead of the February 2016 elections. It looks at the history of elections since the revolution in 1979 and highlights the current intensified infighting among the various factions of the Iranian regime.

IRAN: A Writ of Deception and Cover-up: Iranian Regime's Secret Committee Hid Military Dimensions of its Nuclear Program

February 2016, 30 pages

The book provides details about a top-secret committee in charge of forging the answers to the International Atomic Energy Agency (IAEA) regarding the Possible Military Dimensions (PMD) of Tehran's nuclear program, including those related to the explosive detonators called EBW (Exploding Bridge Wire) detonator, which is an integral part of a program to develop an implosion type nuclear device.

Iranian Regime's Nuclear Duplicity: An Analysis of Tehran's Trickery in Talks with the P 5+1

January 2016, 74 pages

This book examines Iran's behavior throughout the negotiations process in an effort to inform the current dialogue on a potential agreement. Drawing on both publicly available sources and those within Iran, the book focuses on two major periods of intense negotiations with the regime: 2003-2004 and 2013-2015. Based on this evidence, it then extracts the principles and motivations behind Tehran's approach to negotiations as well as the tactics used to trick its counterparts and reach its objectives.

Key to Countering Islamic Fundamentalism: Maryam Rajavi's Testimony To The U.S. House Foreign Affairs Committee

June 2015, 68 pages

Testimony before U.S. House Foreign Affairs Committee's subcommittee on Terrorism, non-Proliferation, and Trade discussing ISIS and Islamic fundamentalism. The book contains Maryam Rajavi's full testimony as well as the question and answer by representatives.

Meet the National Council of Resistance of Iran

June 2014, 150 pages

Meet the National Council of Resistance of Iran discusses what NCRI stands for, what its platform is, what it has done so far, and why a vision for a free, democratic, secular, non-nuclear republic in Iran would serve the world peace.

www.ingramcontent.com/pod-product-compliance
Lightning Source LLC
Chambersburg PA
CBHW041959080526
44588CB00021B/2798